Frances Turnbull

Published by Musicaliti® Publishers
575 Tonge Moor Road, Bolton, BL2 3BN

Copyright © 2016 Musicaliti
ISBN 978-1-907935-74-9

All rights reserved. No part of this publication may be reproduced, stored in a retrieval system, or transmitted by any means, mechanical, photocopying, recording or otherwise, without the prior permission of the copyright holder.

Index of Songs

Aiken Drum	20
Coming Round the Mountain	23
Darling Clementine	19
Drunken Sailor	29
Farmer in the Dell	18
G-Scale	30
Home on the Range	26
Lil Liza Jane	11
London Bridge	14
Love Somebody	17
Muffin Man	22
My Bonnie	21
My Paddle	9
Over in the Meadow	10
Polly put the Kettle on	28
Pretty Little Susie	25
Ring a Rosies	16
Row Row Row	12
This Old Man	15
Twinkle Twinkle	13
What shall we do?	24

Guitar Basics

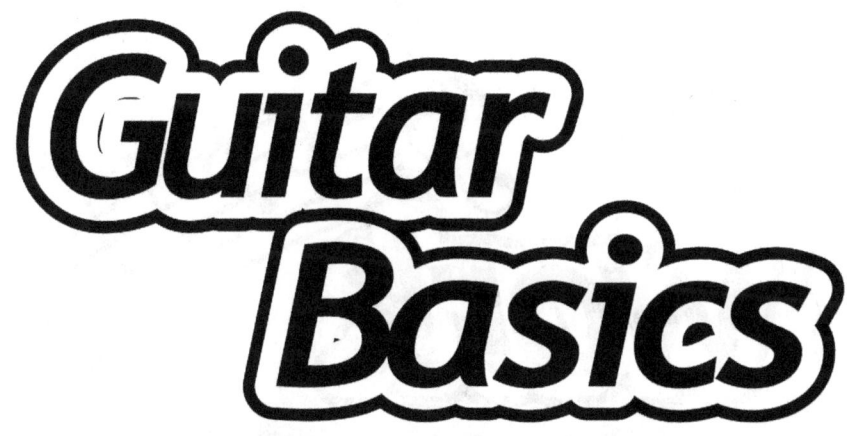

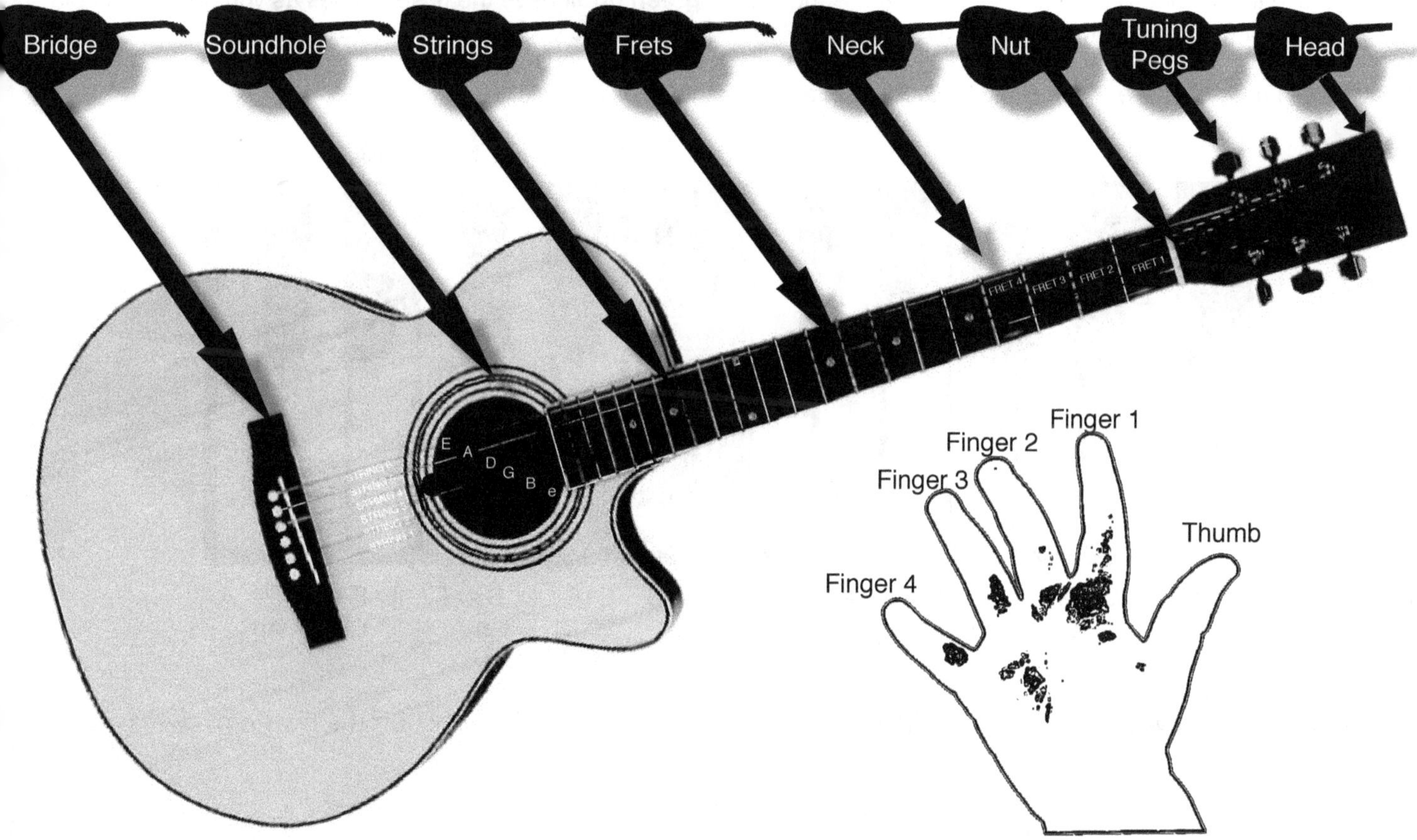

Bridge
Soundhole
Strings
Frets
Neck
Nut
Tuning Pegs
Head
FRET 4
FRET 3
FRET 2
FRET 1
E
A
D
G
B
e
Finger 1
Finger 2
Finger 3
Finger 4
Thumb

2
1
4

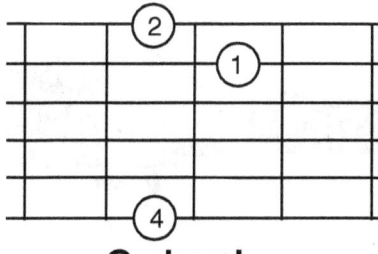

G chord

Guitar can be used to play tunes or **melodies** (one or a few notes at a time) or to accompany songs being sung - by playing all the strings with your fingers in the shape of a chord. The songs in this book are all in the chord of G. This means that you can play the G chord and sing along to the songs, or play the tune - it is a great skill to be able to do both! You could even have a guitar friend play the chord while you play the melody (tune) or the other way around! These pictures show the chords that we have used in this book. The numbers in circles show which finger to use!

3
2
1

C chord

1
3
2

D chord

1
2

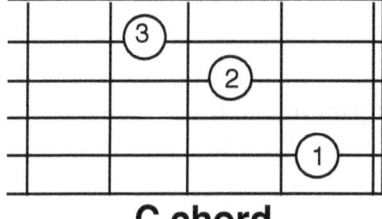

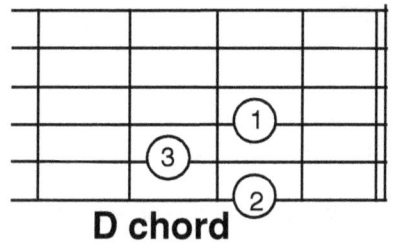

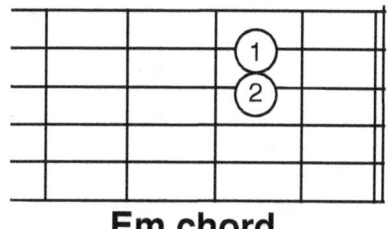

Em chord

How the notes work

The songs in this book are written in the **G scale**. Songs in the **green book** have the fewest notes as you get used to playing the notes of songs on the guitar, with more notes in **pink book**, **yellow book**, **blue book** and **orange book**.

The notes in a G scale are: **G, A, B, C, D, E, F#**. On a **piano**, they look like this:

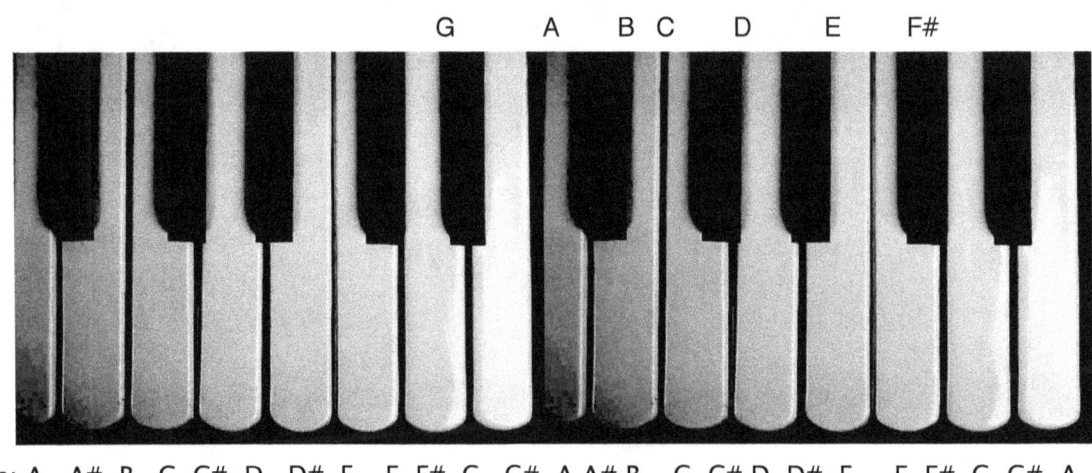

Music notes: A A#/Bb B C C#/Db D D#/Eb E F F#/Gb G G#/Ab A A#/Bb B C C#/Db D D#/Eb E F F#/Gb G G#/Ab A

On a **guitar**, they look like this:
(guitar strings start with different notes/letters, and this picture shows the notes on the E string)

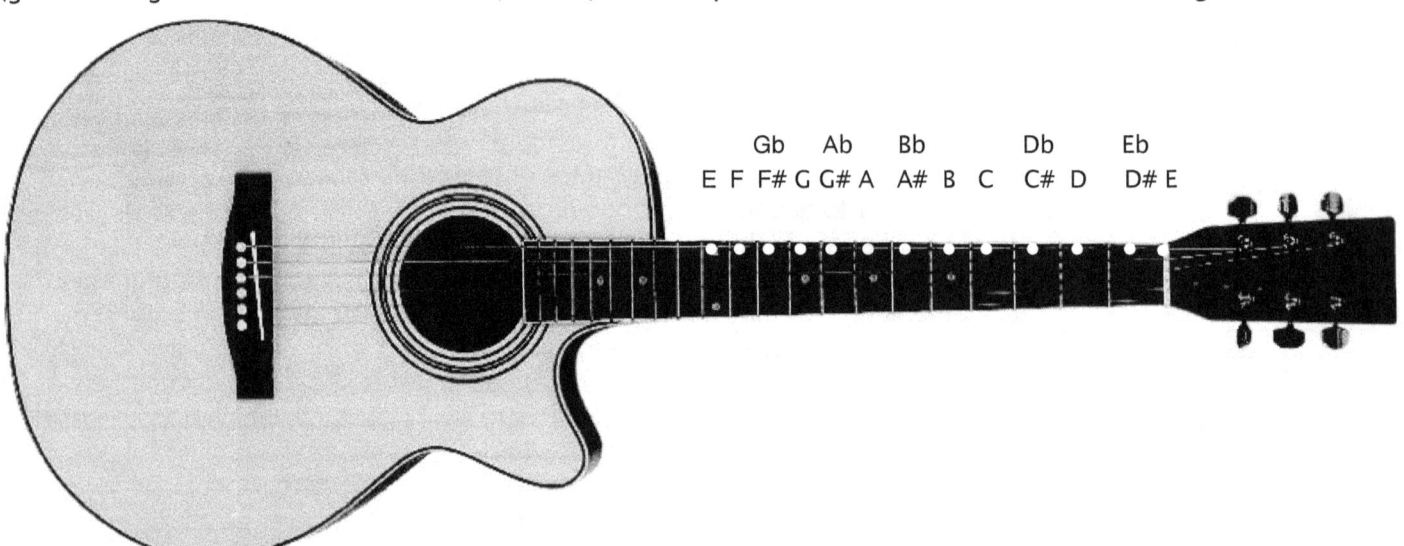

E F F#/Gb G G#/Ab A A#/Bb B C C#/Db D D#/Eb E

Scales have set gaps in between the notes, and the gaps between these notes determine when the black notes, or sharps and flats (also called accidentals) are used. Accidentals can be sharp (#) or flat (b), depending on the scale.

By the end of the **Orange Songs**, you will have played **all** of the notes in the G scale!

How the beats work

It's easy to focus on only playing the right notes, but we need to get the **long and short** beats right, too. It can be tricky to work out until we know what the lines and holes in the notes mean, so we can use **movement words** to remember how the beats sound. That way, you could say the movement words instead of the song words to remember how long to play the note!

Semibreve/Whole Note
VERY SLOW WALK
(4 beats)

Minim/Half Note
SLOW WALK
(2 beats)

Crotchet/Quarter Note
WALK
(1 beat)

Quaver/Eighth Note
JOGGING
(half of a beat)

Semiquaver/Sixteenth Note
JOGGING QUICKLY
(quarter of a beat)

Dotted quaver-semiquaver /
Dotted eighth note sixteenth note
SKIPPING
(short-long)

Semiquaver-dotted quaver /
Sixteenth note dotted eighth note
GALLOP
(long-short)

Quaver semiquaver /
Eighth note-sixteenth note
"HAMBURGER"
(slow-quick-quick)

Semiquaver-quaver /
Sixteenth note-eighth note
"SAUSAGES"
(quick-quick slow)

Repeat the part between these signs

For example, if we sang the movement rhythms to "This Old Man", we would have:

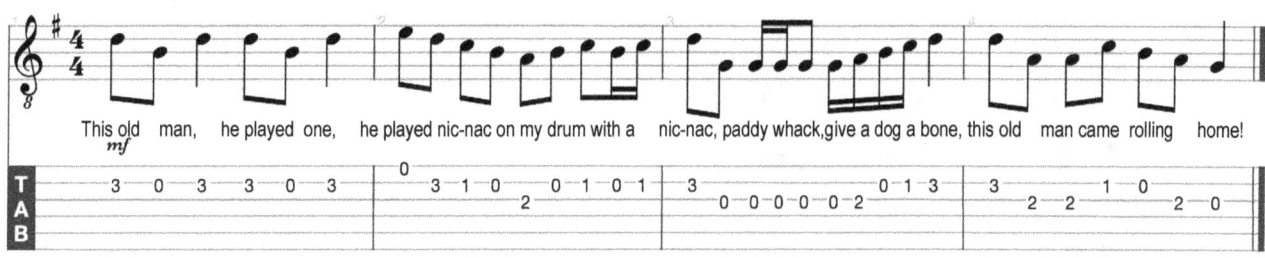

Give it a try before singing the songs!

7

Orange Songs

These pages introduce songs with 6 to 9 notes, and the different lengths of beats used:

E is on the 1st open string
D is on the 2nd string, 3rd fret
C is on the 2nd string, 1st fret
B is on the 2nd open string
A is on the 3rd string, 2nd fret
G is on the 3rd open string
F# is on the 4th string, 4th fret
E is on the 4th string, 2nd fret
D is on the 4th open string

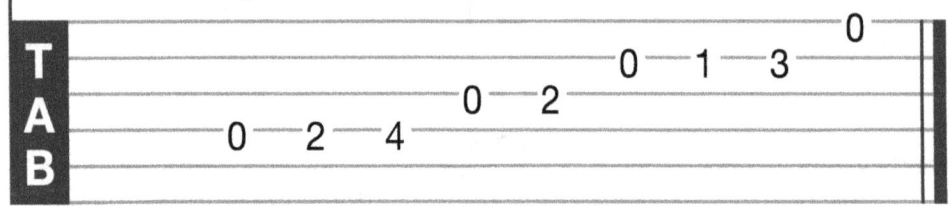

1st string
2nd string
3rd string
4th string
5th string
6th string

Semibreve/Whole Note
VERY SLOW WALK
(4 beats)

Minim/Half Note
SLOW WALK
(2 beats)

Crotchet/Quarter Note
WALK
(1 beat)

Quaver/Eighth Note
JOGGING
(half of a beat)

Semiquaver/Sixteenth Note
JOGGING QUICKLY
(quarter of a beat)

*Dotted quaver-semiquaver /
Dotted eighth note sixteenth note*
SKIPPING
(short-long)

*Semiquaver-dotted quaver /
Sixteenth note dotted eighth note*
GALLOP
(long-short)

*Quaver semiquaver /
Eighth note-sixteenth note*
"HAMBURGER"
(slow-quick-quick)

*Semiquaver-quaver /
Sixteenth note-eighth note*
"SAUSAGES"
(quick-quick slow)

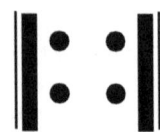

Repeat the part between these signs

Over in the Meadow

Traditional

Guitar Standard Tuning
E-A-D-G-B-E
♩ = 120

O - ver in the meadow in the sand, in the sun, lived an old, mo - ther ti - ger and her lit - tle ti - ger one, "ROAR" said the mo - ther, "I ROAR!" said the one, so they roared and they roar - ed in the sa - nd, in the sun!

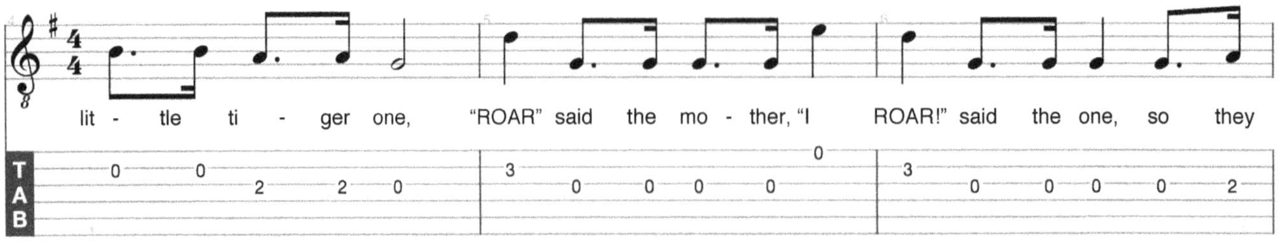

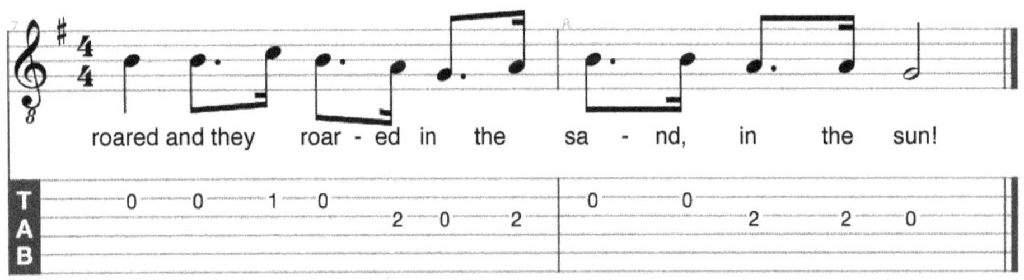

Next verse:

**Over in the meadow where the stream runs so blue
Was an old mother elephant and her little calves two
"Stomp," said the mother, "we stomp," said the two
So they stomped and they stomped where the stream runs so blue**

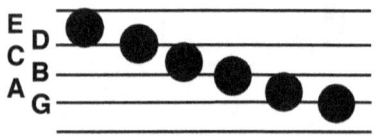

10

Guitar Standard Tuning
E-A-D-G-B-E
♩ = 180

Traditional

I know a girl that you don't know, Lil' Li - za Jane,

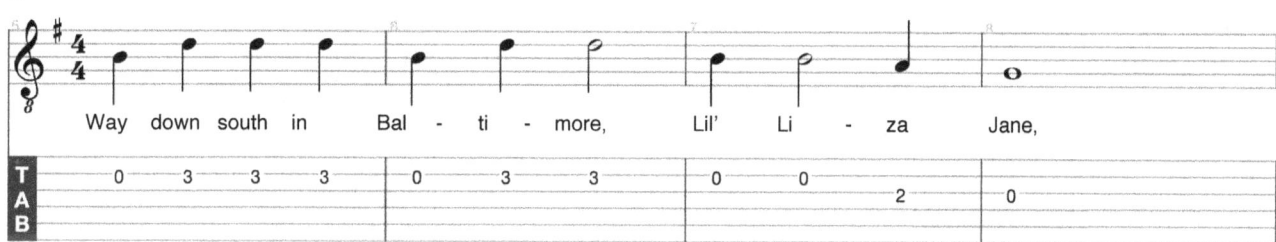

Way down south in Bal - ti - more, Lil' Li - za Jane,

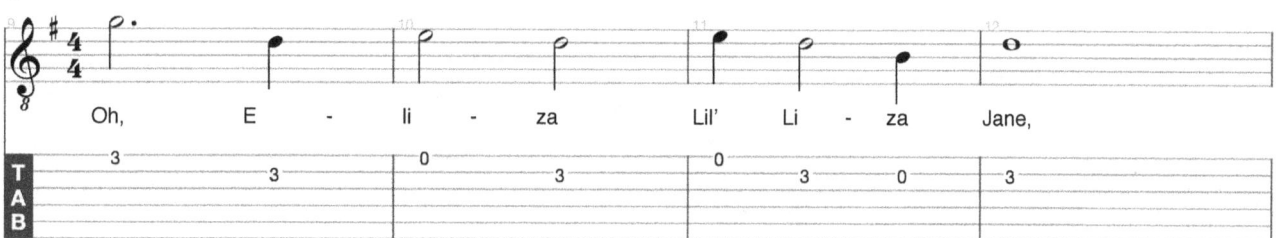

Oh, E - li - za Lil' Li - za Jane,

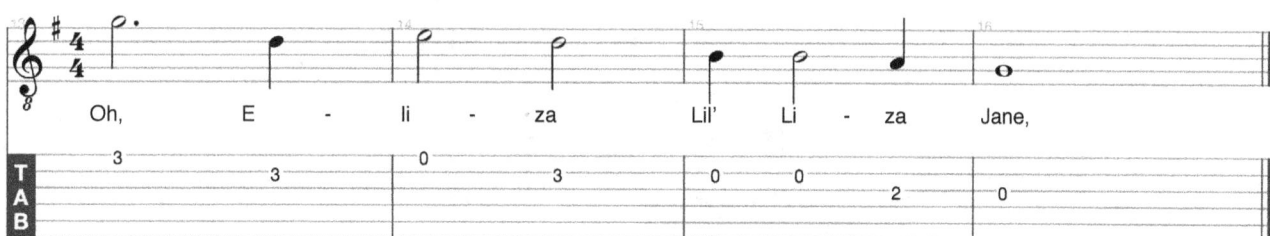

Oh, E - li - za Lil' Li - za Jane,

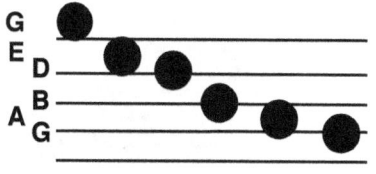

Guitar Standard Tuning
E-A-D-G-B-E
♩ = 120

Traditional

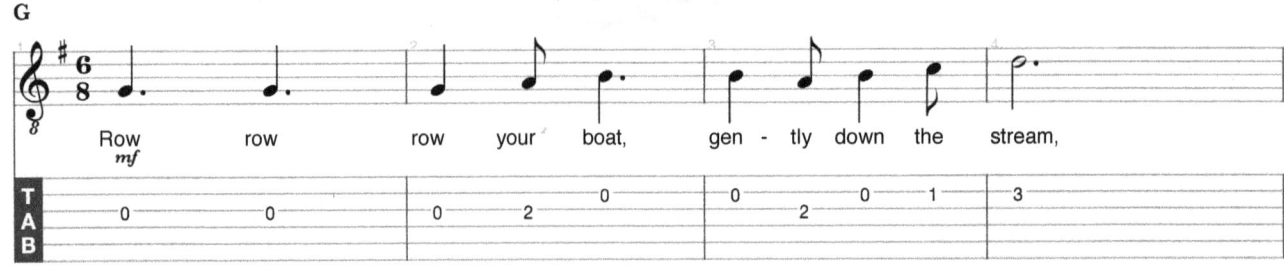

Row row row your boat, gen - tly down the stream,

Mer - ri - ly, mer - ri - ly, mer - ri - ly, mer - ri - ly, life is but a dream!

Next verse:

Row, row, row your boat
Gently down the stream
If you see a crocodile
Don't forget to scream

Row, row, row your boat
Gently to the shore
If you see a lion
Don't forget to ROAR!

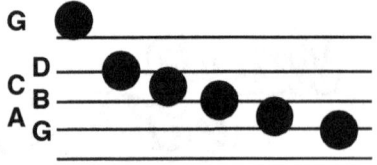

Guitar Standard Tuning
E-A-D-G-B-E
♩ = 120

Traditional

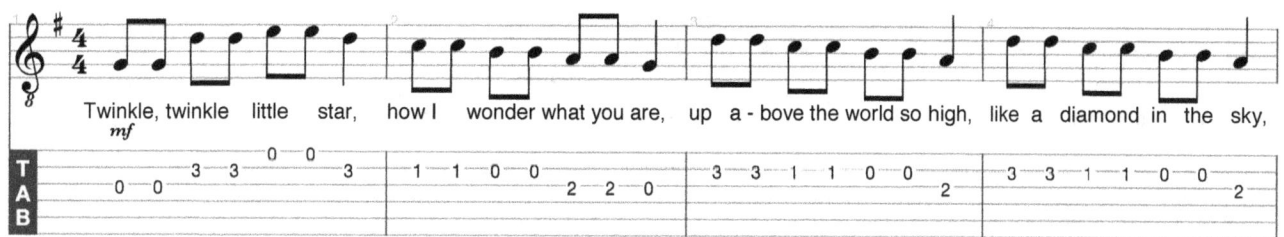

Twinkle, twinkle little star, how I wonder what you are, up a-bove the world so high, like a diamond in the sky,

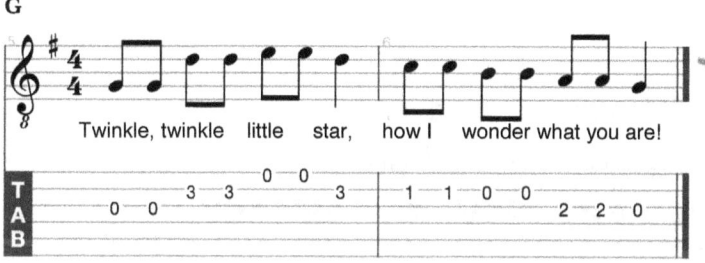

Twinkle, twinkle little star, how I wonder what you are!

Next verse:

When the blazing sun has gone
When he nothing shines upon
Then you show your little light
Twinkle, twinkle through the night
Twinkle, twinkle little star
How I wonder what you are

In the dark blue sky so deep
Through my curtains often peep
For you never close your eyes
Til the morning sun does rise
Twinkle, twinkle little star
How I wonder what you are

13

London Bridge

Traditional

Guitar Standard Tuning
E-A-D-G-B-E
♩ = 120

London bridge is falling down, falling down, falling down, London bridge is falling down, my fair la - dy!

Next verse:

Build it up with wood and clay
Wood and clay, wood and clay
Build it up with wood and clay, my fair lady

Wood and clay will wash away
Wash away, wash away
Wood and clay will wash away, my fair lady

Build it up with bricks and mortar
Bricks and mortar, bricks and mortar
Build it up with bricks and mortar, my fair lady

Build it up with iron and steel
Iron and steel, iron and steel
Build it up with iron and steel, my fair lady

Build it up with silver and gold
Silver and gold, silver and gold
Build it up with silver and gold, my fair lady

  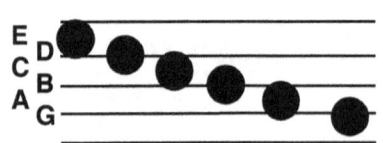

Guitar Standard Tuning
E-A-D-G-B-E
♩ = 120

Traditional

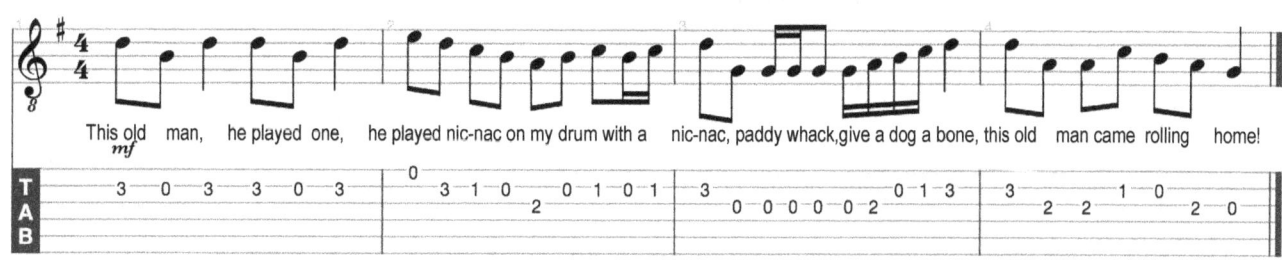

Next verse:

This old man, he played two, he played nicnac on my shoe
With a nicnac paddy whack, give a dog a bone
This old man came rolling home

This old man, he played three, he played nicnac on my knee
With a nicnac paddy whack, give a dog a bone
This old man came rolling home

This old man, he played four, he played nicnac on my door
With a nicnac paddy whack, give a dog a bone
This old man came rolling home

This old man, he played five, he played nicnac on my hive
With a nicnac paddy whack, give a dog a bone
This old man came rolling home

This old man, he played six, he played nicnac on my sticks
With a nicnac paddy whack, give a dog a bone
This old man came rolling home

Ring a Rosies

Guitar Standard Tuning
E-A-D-G-B-E
♩ = 120

Traditional

G

Ring a ring a ro-sies a pocket full of po-sies a-ti-shoo a-ti-shoo, we all fall down!

Watch Out! ♩ ♩ ♫

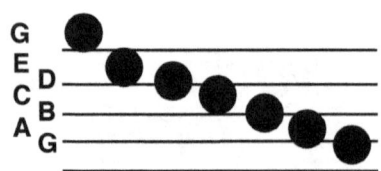

Traditional

Guitar Standard Tuning
E-A-D-G-B-E
♩ = 120

Next verse:

Love somebody
Yes I do
Love somebody
Yes I do
Love somebody
Yes I do
Love somebody
But I won't say who!

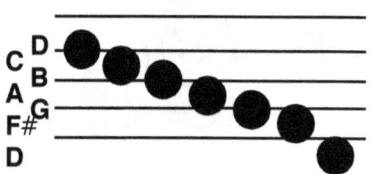

Guitar Standard Tuning
E-A-D-G-B-E
♩ = 200

Traditional

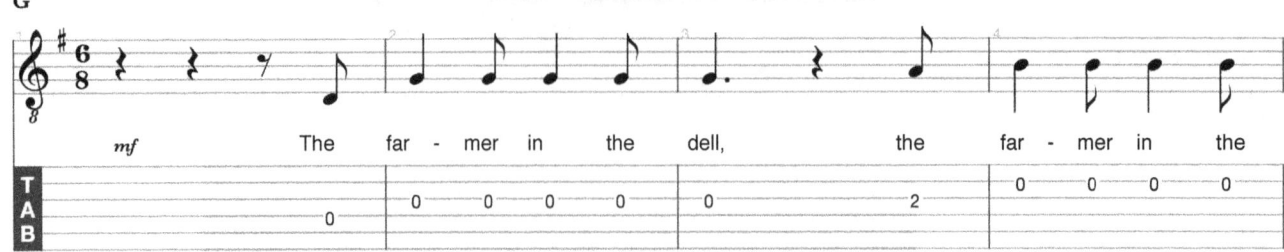

mf The far-mer in the dell, the far-mer in the

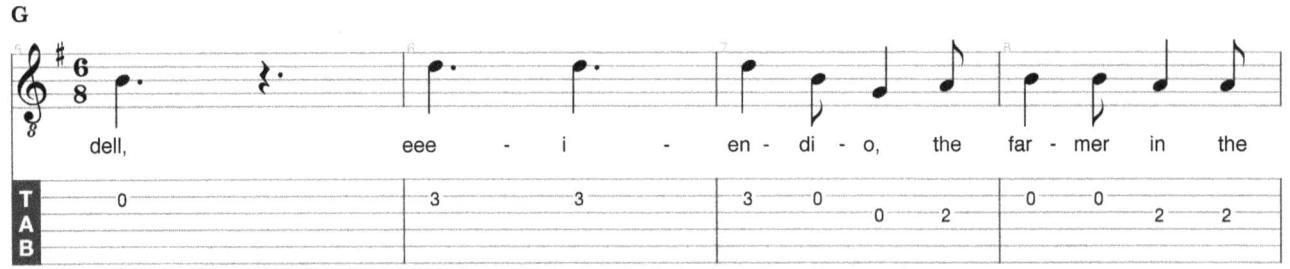

dell, eee - i - en - di - o, the far-mer in the

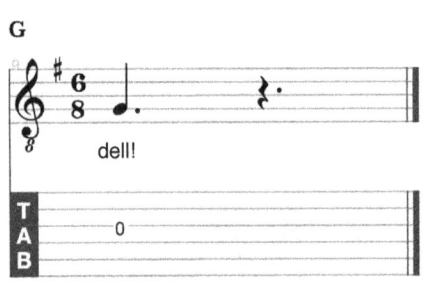

dell!

Next verse:

The farmer has a wife, the farmer has a wife, E-I-N-D-O ...
The wife has a child, the wife has a child, E-I-N-D-O ...
The child has a dog, the child has a dog, E-I-N-D-O ...
The dog has a cat, the dog has a cat, E-I-N-D-O ...
The cat has a mouse, the cat has a mouse, E-I-N-D-O ...
The mouse has a cheese, the mouse has a cheese, E-I-N-D-O ...
We all pat the cheese, we all pat the cheese, E-I-N-D-O ...

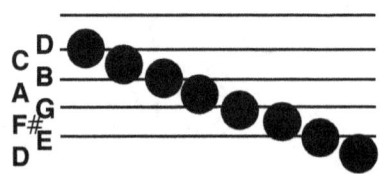

Guitar Standard Tuning
E-A-D-G-B-E
♩ = 120

Traditional

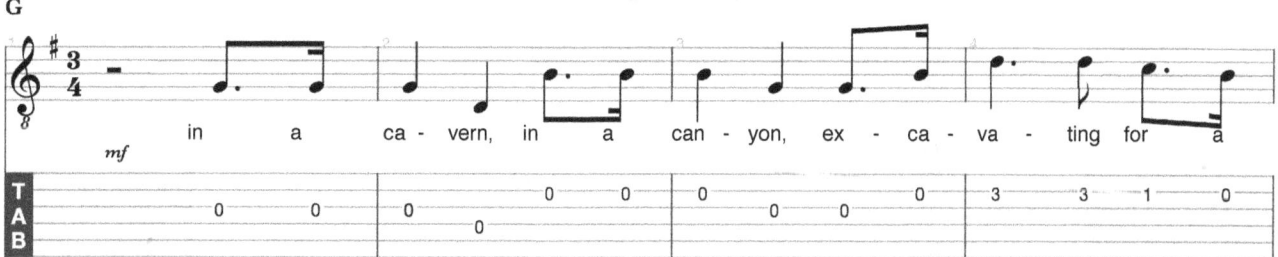
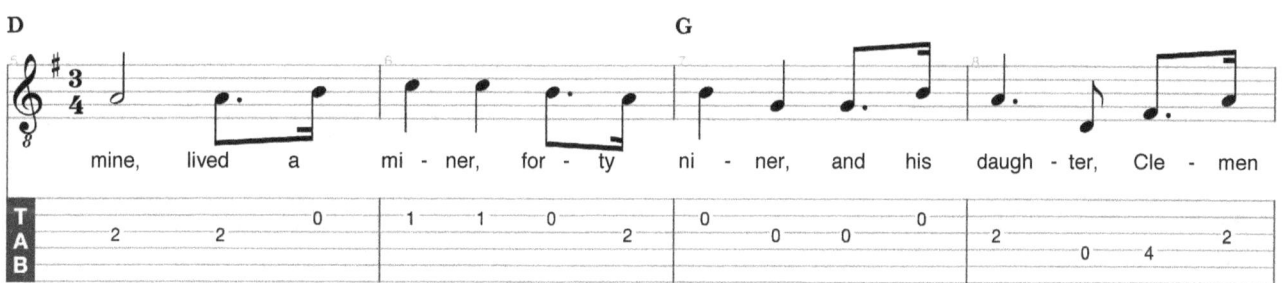
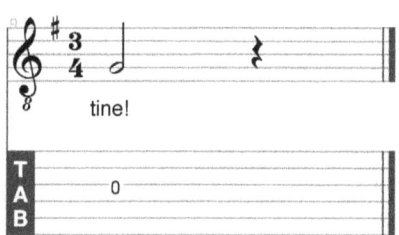

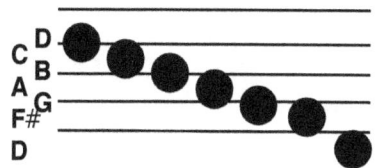

Aiken Drum

Traditional

Guitar Standard Tuning
E-A-D-G-B-E
♩ = 120

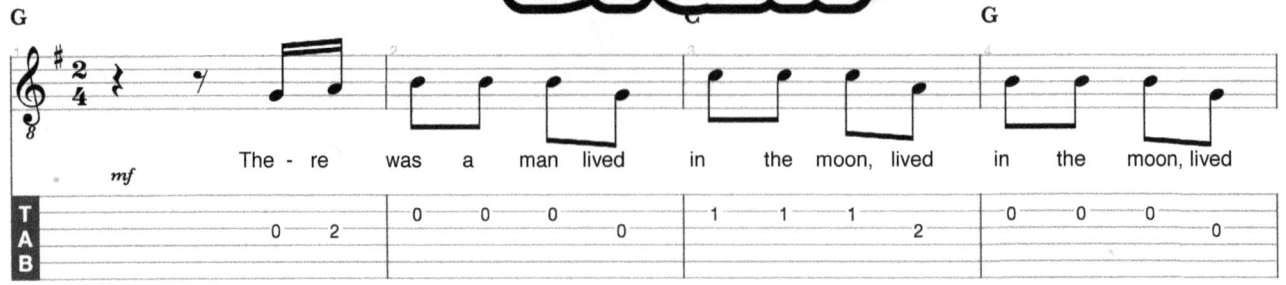
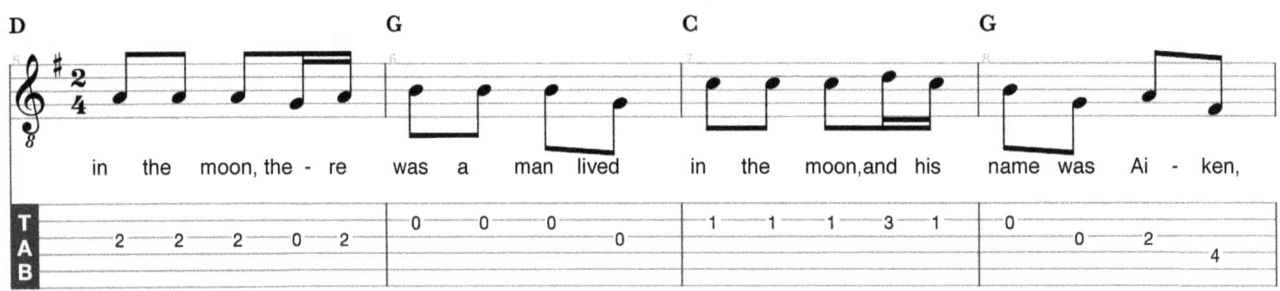
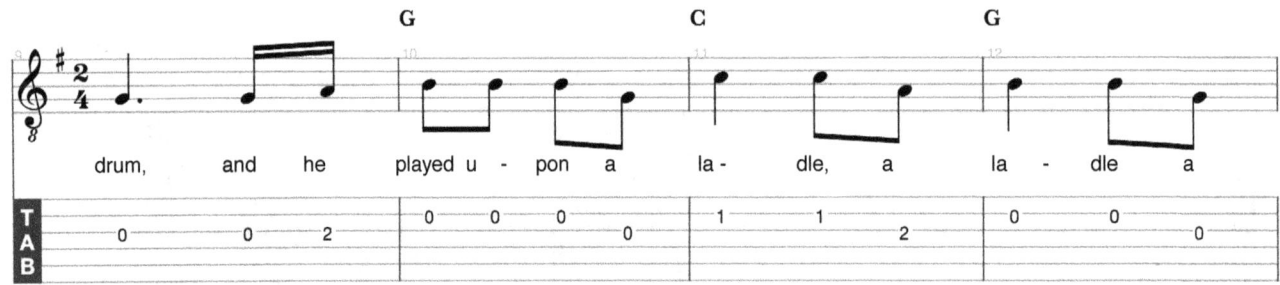
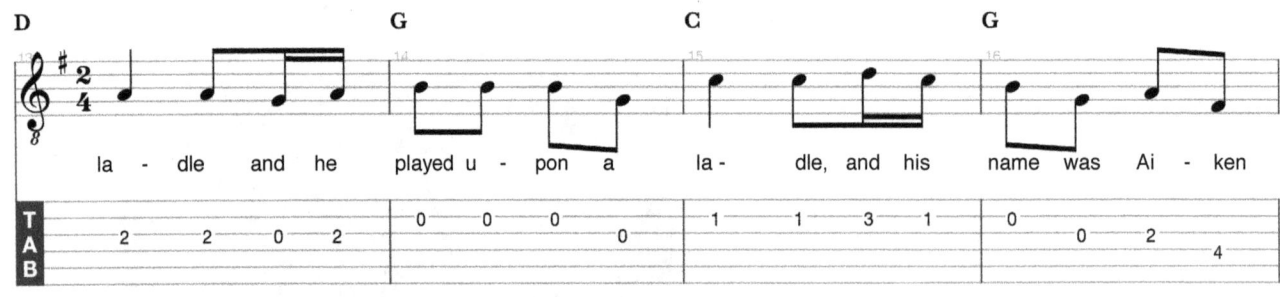

My Bonnie

Traditional

Guitar Standard Tuning
E-A-D-G-B-E
♩ = 120

Oh blow you waves over the ocean
Oh blow you waves over the sea
Oh blow you waves over the ocean
And bring back my Bonnie to me

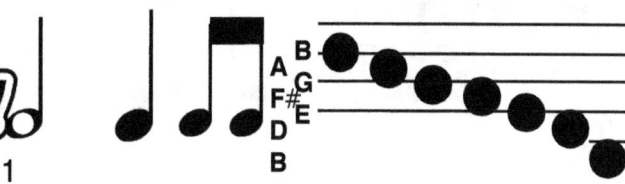

Muffin Man

Traditional

Guitar Standard Tuning
E-A-D-G-B-E
♩ = 120

Do you know the muf-fin man, the muf-fin man, the muf-fin man, do you know the muf-fin man who Lives on Dru-ry Lane?

Next verse:

Yes I know the muffin man
The muffin man, the muffin man
Yes I know the muffin man
Who lives on Drury Lane

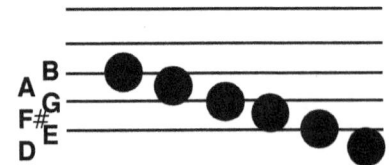

What shall we do?

Traditional

Guitar Standard Tuning
E-A-D-G-B-E

♩ = 200

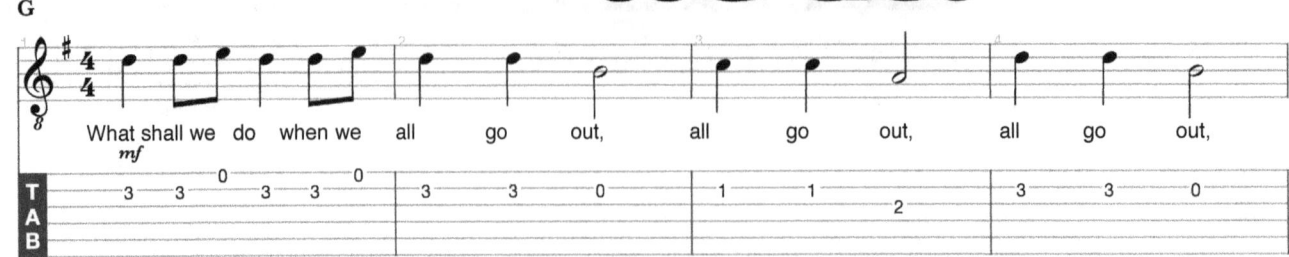

What shall we do when we all go out, all go out, all go out,

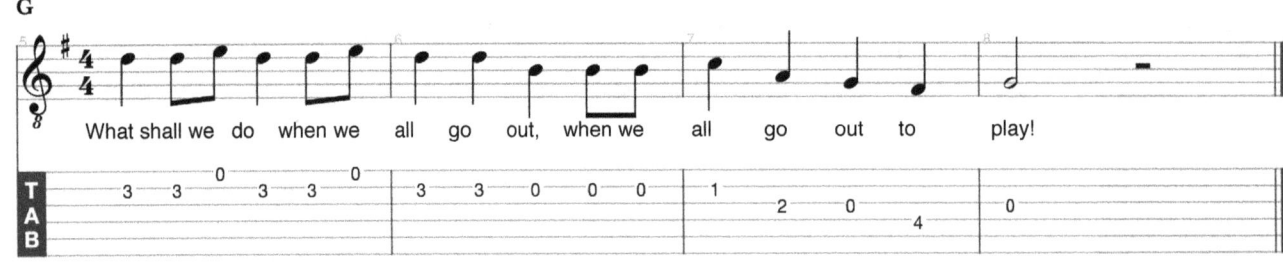

What shall we do when we all go out, when we all go out to play!

Next verse:

Let's all play on the merry-go-round
The merry-go-round, the merry-go-round
Let's all play on the merry-go-round
When we all go out to play

Let's all play on the see saw
The see saw, the see saw
Let's all play on the see saw
When we all go out to play

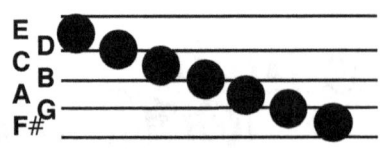

Home on the Range

Traditional

Guitar Standard Tuning
E-A-D-G-B-E
♩ = 120

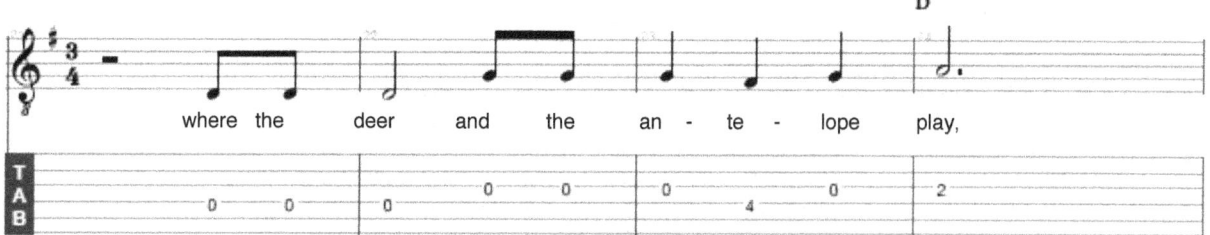
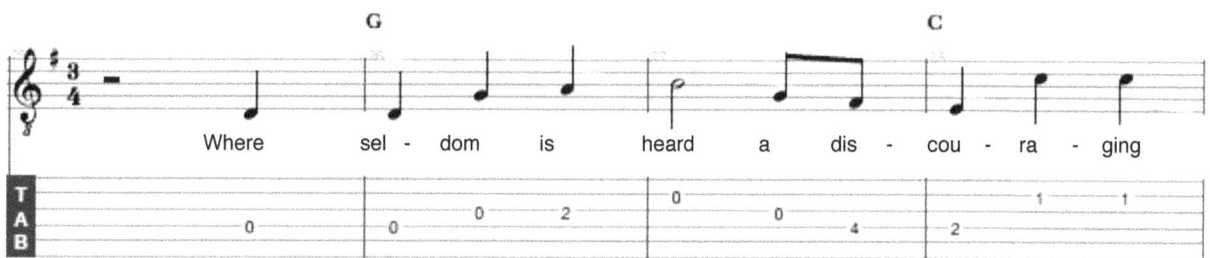

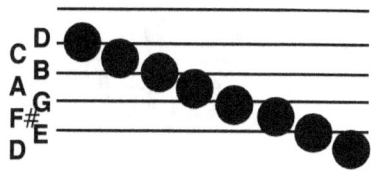

Polly put the Kettle on

Guitar Standard Tuning
E-A-D-G-B-E
♩ = 120

Traditional

G D G

Pol-ly put the ket-tle on, Pol-ly put the ket-tle on, Pol-ly put the ket-tle on, we'll all have tea!

mf

Next verse:

Sukey take it off again
Sukey take it off again
Sukey take it off again
They've all gone away

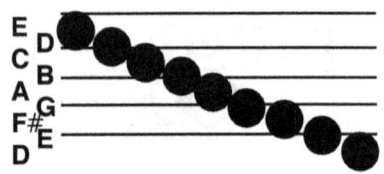

Guitar Standard Tuning
E-A-D-G-B-E

♩ = 200

Traditional

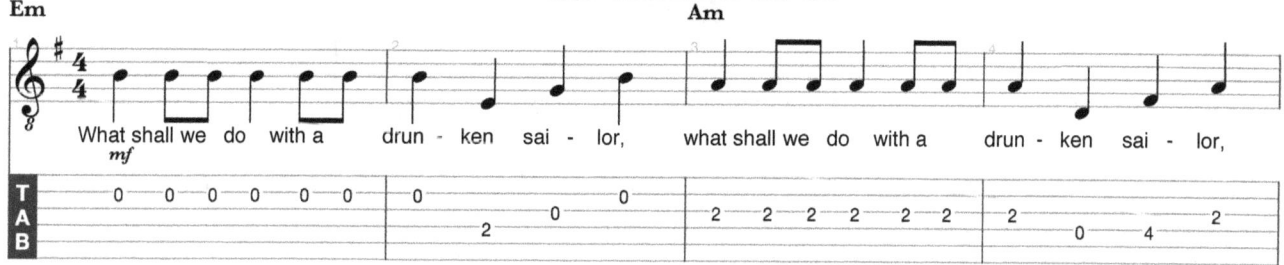

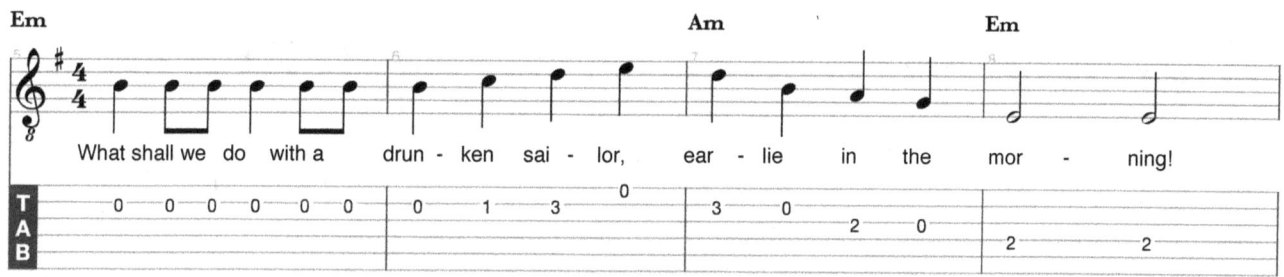

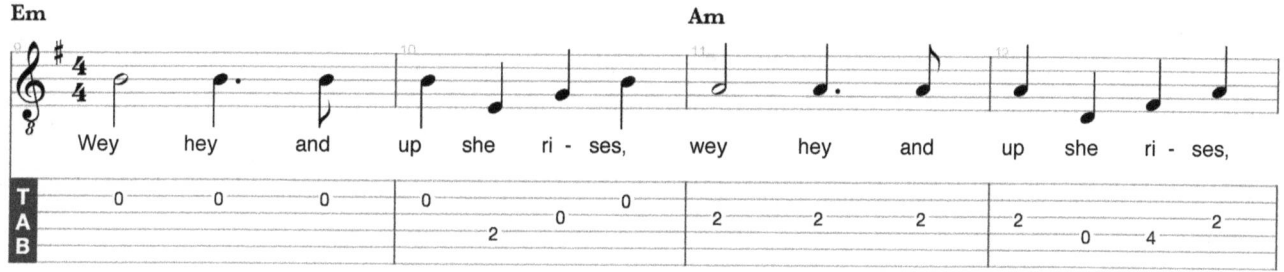

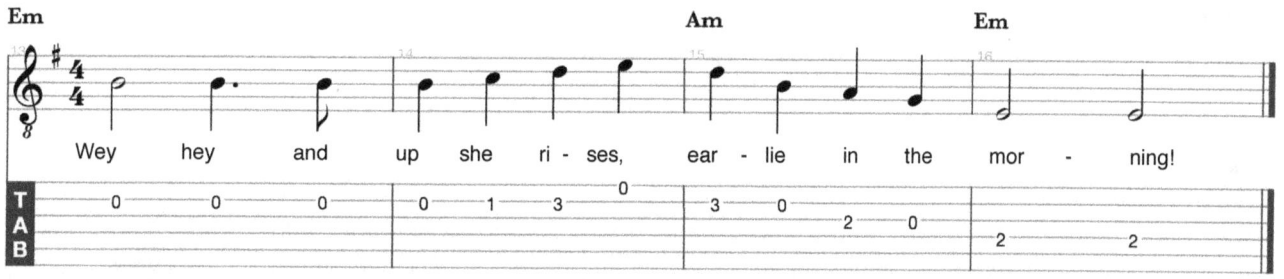

Make him work and make him bail her
Make him work and make him bail her
Make him work and make him bail her
Earlie in the morning

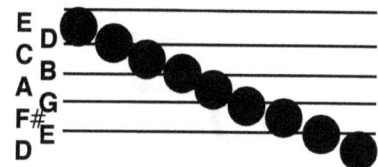

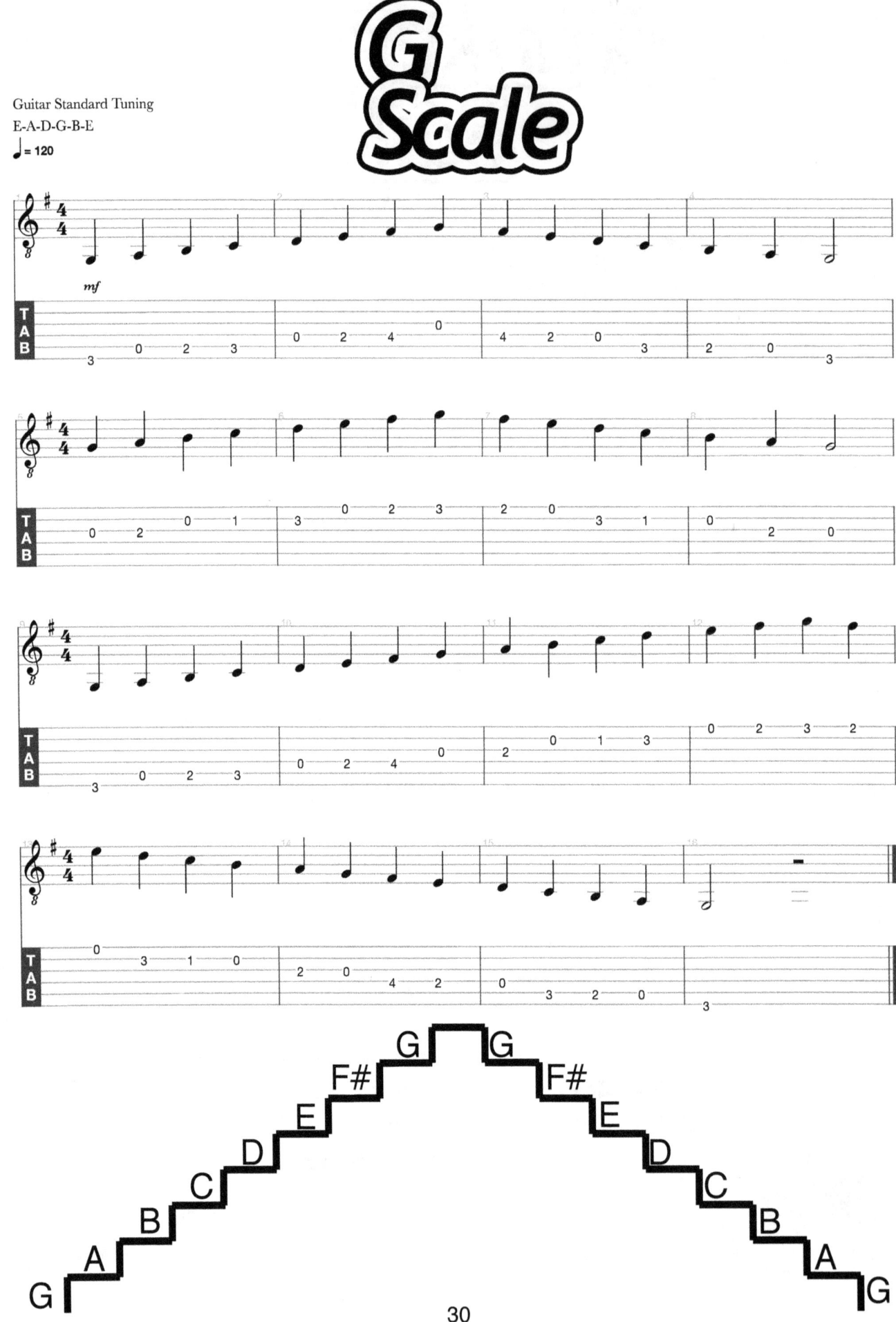

ABOUT THE AUTHOR

Frances has presented early years music sessions in a variety of settings since 2006, after training as a secondary mathematics and science teacher. She is fascinated by research into the health, educational and developmental benefits of music. Not content with being involved with children's music alone, she directs a local community choir, the Warblers.

AVAILABLE TITLES:

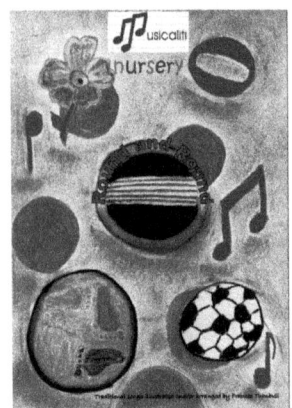

Musicaliti Nursery: Round and Round is a full-colour, illustrated book of well known children's songs for children. Each song includes music rhythms to which children can clap, tap, walk and sing.
ISBN: 978-1-907-935-008

Musicaliti Nursery Series: Magical Musical Kingdom is a full-colour, teaching series of well known and original children's songs with a royal element. Sessions include suggested instruments and activities, with an optional CD of music to purchase or download.
ISBN: 978-1-907-935-152

Musicaliti Nursery Series: Sharks, Fish, Shells is a full-colour, teaching series of well known and original children's songs with a fishy element. Sessions include suggested instruments and activities, with an optional CD of music to purchase or download.
ISBN: 978-1-907-935-169

Musicaliti Nursery Series: Yum, Yum, Yum! is a full-colour, teaching series of well known and original children's songs with a foody element. Sessions include suggested instruments and activities, with an optional CD of music to purchase or download.
ISBN: 978-1-907-935-206

Musicaliti Music Gone Wild is a full-colour, teaching series of well known and original children's songs with an animal element. Using ukulele instruction and chords, play along with your favourite animal songs today!

ISBN: 978-1-907-935-688

Musicaliti Goodies for Guitar is a full-colour, teaching series of well known and original children's songs for beginner guitar. With 90 songs both familiar and unfamiliar, this book covers songs in the scale of G, providing music notation, tablature and guitar chords for accompaniment.
ISBN: 978-1-907-935-206

FORTHCOMING TITLES:

Musicaliti Nursery Series: Balloons, Candles, Cake is a full-colour, teaching series of well known and original children's songs with a party element. Sessions include suggested instruments and activities, with an optional CD of music to purchase or download.
ISBN: 978-1-907-935-190

Musicaliti Nursery Series: Car, bike, plane is a full-colour, teaching series of well known and original children's songs with a transport element. Sessions include suggested instruments and activities, with an optional CD of music to purchase or download.

ISBN: 978-1-907-935-213

Follow Musicaliti NOW on FaceBook, LInkedIn, ReverbNation, SoundCloud, Twitter and YouTube!

www.ingramcontent.com/pod-product-compliance
Lightning Source LLC
Chambersburg PA
CBHW081503040426
42446CB00016B/3375